Glimpses Beyond

A Poetic Collection

with

Photographic Selections

C. Geordie Campbell

Glimpses Beyond

A Poetic Collection

by Rev. Dr. Charles Geordie Campbell

Copyright © 2023

ISBN: 979-889074905-5

Any use of these materials requires proper attribution.

All rights reserved.

Gorham Printing, Inc., 3718 Mahoney Drive

Centralia, Washington 98531

Geordie Campbell
55 Creeks Edge Drive
Saco, Maine 04072
860-878-4197
cgc.pastor.emeritus@gmail.com

Also by Geordie Campbell

The Heart of the Story
(2018)

Lights Leading Home
(2021)

Tell Me with a Story
Narrative Prompts for Seeking Souls
(2022)

As You May Become
Living into Faith
(2023)

Photograph on front and rear cover:

"Green Pastures, Still Waters"
Geordie Campbell ~ Weston, Vermont
August 2015

Table of Contents

Whispering River
Up There
Dark November
The Owl's Call
Mortality
What Turtles Teach
Hey Old Friend
Liberty's Vision
Fallow
Still Working
Jet Blue 533
Contradiction
Winter: Drifting Paths
Spring: Intimations of Heaven
Summer: Crickets and Cicadas
Autumn: Yellow Blaze and Gold
Fireside
Vapor Trails
Grace Arriving
Jig Saw
Snow Day
Joy Is Like
Kennebunk Air
Autumn Again
Nostalgia
Woke
Packing

Beachcomb
Seasonal Misery
Waiting
Preference
Whole Body Wags
The Moment Is Now
Life Opens Free
It Looks Different
The Other Side
Sabbath Whisper
This Is the Day
In The Leaving
Increments
Shelf Life
The Silent Asking
To Simply Receive
Harvest at Harpswell
Clarity
Watching Over
When Life Says No
A Deeper More
I Wonder
My Lucky Day
Ruach
Earth's Turning
Birthday Card
Mind Fog
Exposure
The Rim of the Day
A New Day Dawning

Glimpses Beyond

Rabbi Abraham Joshua Heschel once wrote: "God is not always silent, and people are not always blind. In every person's life there are moments when there is a lifting of the veil at the horizon of the known, opening a glimpse of the eternal."

He was so right. I can attest to this in my own life. Instances and insights have come along for me and have pointed beyond to the More and Deeper of God. Most often they are unexpected and unbidden. Best of all, sometimes I have the good sense to pay attention!

Celtic Spirituality has long held that there are "thin places" wherein the separation of the material and spiritual dimensions in life seems thin and nearly imperceptible. Imagine a veil between this world that we know and master so well, and another world that we only have hunches and hopes about. At such times we can almost reach across from one to the other.

Paul Tillich adds more yet again. "Here and there in the world, and now and then in our lives, something of God brushes close." He called these glimpses of "the eternal now" in which we become aware of the depth and height of life in new and present ways – moments of something quite timeless yet held in the bonds of time.

This small volume is a gathering of just such glimpses. They run the gamut: the mystery of the sky, the wagging of a tail, the power of nature, the turn of the seasons, the anguish of loss, the blessing of clean windows, the experience of growing older, the taste of fresh fruit. And so very much more.

Along your own "here and there, then and now" experiences - your "thin places" - may these words and images inspire and question, affirm and empower, provoke and plant. And may they open glimpses of beyond in your own moments of life's invitation.

In the fullness of blessing,

Geordie Campbell

Saco, Maine   ~   May 2023

"A Thin Place, Newly Defined!"   Higgin's Beach, Maine   June 2020

Whispering River

The river whispered in currents deep beneath my kayak.

"Upstream first. Go where the water is coming from.
But claim your stride quickly,
or any gain will be lost as I go my way."

So, I paddled hard and determined.

In a little while she whispered again.

"Now stop. Breathe my moist air. Relax. Let yourself drift.
I'll carry you from here."

An invisible moment turned the movement of my boat
upstream to down - as if being pulled by liquid gravity.

Before long I was back where I began, enlivened by my journey
and glad I had listened to the river's voice.

Upstream then down, paddle then pause, effort then ease.
Amazing what rivers have to say
to those who listen.

"Whispering River"   Weatogue, Connecticut   July 2012

Up There

A thousand pieces of sky
move briskly in the summer air;
clouds in towering billows
silhouetted against deep blue.

She has become my friend,
inviting me with awe and mystery
not because I imagine "up there"
versus "down here" but for
the mystical wondering
to the far edges and beyond.

Among the treasures in Dad's passing:
I am more acutely aware of the
heights and depths of life;
persuaded that God holds all of it,
on this side of our earthly journeys
and the other for those gone home.

Every bit, in every season; beyond all
thought of time, the cycles of aging
and life carry us over the years,
all the way to the heart of holy promise.

"Wild Summer Skies"   Ludlow, Vermont   August 2011

Dark November

Who can forget
how suffocating and
absolute the grief?

Winsome Jack,
adoring first lady,
a plaza corner turned.

America lost something
of her soul
that Dallas day.

I can only speak for me,
ten years old. but wounded
in my own wordless way,

afraid to sleep in the dark
with my closet door closed
anymore.

written on the 50th anniversary
of John F. Kennedy's death.

"Light Matters"　　　Iona, Scotland　　　April 2010

The Owl's Call

An owl startled me to waking,
filling up the darkness with her song.

Hauntingly beautiful 'til break of day,
but beautifully haunting, too.

An indigenous story came to my mind:
"I Heard the Owl Call My Name."

It places the owl as the harbinger of death,
calling out the next one to cross over.

I listened intently, pondering such intuitive
and natural ways of understanding.

Whose name was at the center of her singing?
Was it mine, or one nearby whom I love?

Or was it only a song reminding me
that one day the time of awakening will not rise?

Mortality

I stood on fresh Granby earth today
to lay to rest a dear woman
of ninety-three years.

The eyes of her widower,
ninety-three-plus, were pensive and trusting
as he watched my lips move
with the assurance of the ages.
"Earth to earth, ashes to ashes, dust to dust
is our way of going home."

How haunting to wonder
what will be as the last breath passes,
in that twinkling of an eye,
when the trumpet sounds
and deep gladness is all around,
and heaven is revealed in plain sight.

Of this I am sure: We all will die.
But this none of us know: What will be.
Probably best for now to leave it unknown.

What Turtles Teach

It was a Friday morning, my day off, and one filled with the glory of early autumn. I slid my kayak into the Farmington River at the north end of Simsbury and began to paddle upstream to the south. I set a goal for myself, which was to make journey all the way to the old sycamore and then back in the two hours I had.

And so, I paddled fast and furious. I counted strokes as I pressed on toward the destination. Before long I became single-minded and focused on the goal. It was a race against my day, and I was going to win!

Around about halfway, somewhere in the middle, something caught me off-guard and changed how the balance of my voyage would be spent. I rounded a small bend in the river only to come upon an old log in the water with four beautiful turtles basking in the sun. Their necks were fully extended just to catch the warmth of the rays. I was awestruck at the display of nature's delight.

I ceased my paddle instantly because I didn't want to scare them. And then, by my becoming silent and attentive, came another surprise. A great blue heron took to flight from the river's edge. It flew with majesty and precision, gliding inches off the water all the way down the river until the bend beyond my sight.

As I watched the heron disappear and turned back to the turtles, I found myself wondering how much of the experience of the river I had been passing by unknowing, how much of the morning to which I had been oblivious, all for the goal and the destination.

"Sun Soaking"   Farmington, Connecticut   September 2013

Hey, Old Friend

She was known to me as I was to her
so we needed no ritual of greeting.

The sand, the surf, the gulls hunting
for breakfast, the ocean breeze

connected us to times gone by,
different occasions, other beaches.

I welcomed a sigh, "Hey, old friend."
As always, she was without words.

We picked up where once we left off.
Some relationships are like that.

"Early Morning Mist"   Scarborough, Maine   June 2020

17

"Quiet Souls"   Kennebunkport, Maine   November 2020

"It's been a while," I spoke quietly,
"and life has been complicated and busy."

She listened as if receiving a prayer -
which we both knew she was.

I placed all that I was carrying inside
on her wet sand and misty air.

A simple walk with the Source of Life
who always knows my thoughts.

And one slow step at a time
the Ocean and I reconnected.

Liberty's Vision
(a prayer for July 4th)

Eternal Maker of all nations
and true Heart of every people,
give pause with us today as
we search for words to express
the profound seeds of patriotism
that root deep within us.

Seeds that are far from the narrow
confines of nationalism, and distant
from any boasting of pride or power:
but seeds of love, humble patriotic love,
love that sees and believes in America's
better angels and gleaming vision.

The world is imperfect, as are all of
us in this land of plenty, and there is
much room for repair and improvement.
But do not, therefore, let us be silent
about our gratitude – for liberty, justice,
equality and sweet freedom's call.

Do not let us live or act as if
we are simply entitled to these gifts;
rather, let us resolve to celebrate the vision
we have yet to fully embody,
and to give thanks for blessings
we have yet to fully share.

Look lovingly upon us we pray,
and upon America, and upon

all the people of your world
that one day, by our labor and
to our surprise, peace will be known,
all-in-all, around this precious earth.

May it be so. Amen

"Painful Reflection"   Korean War Memorial   Washington, DC   May 2005

Fallow

Give the soil a rest.
Furrow but don't plant.
Let the ground be still.

Stalks and roots absorb
in silence what only
time can restore.

Earth will be ready
to spout seeds again
after a quiescent season.

I do not fallow well.
Metrics to quantify distract me
from the long harvest.

An old ethic planted soul-deep
does not easily mingle with
fields left untended.

Still Working

Early day, as sun spreads
light across the shadows, it occurs
that while I was sleeping
the sun was still working: warming,
lighting, revealing other lands.

And then I watch the shoreline nearby
as waters rise and fall with tides
that never stopped
across the bridge of night,
still ebbing as earth turns.

I wonder, too, of seeds growing
in the soil of nature's cycles.
Does the darkness work its power
as light and water and nutrients do?
Still working, never resting, never getting tired?

What is for the sun, still shining when I cannot see;
and the tides, rising and ebbing without a fuss;
and the seeds, reaching through the dark soil
is so for God. Mostly God. Especially God.
Still working, never stopping, even at rest.

JetBlue 533

I am sitting on JetBlue flight 533. It's the usual boarding process as people scrunch over-sized-carry-on bags into the bins above. Time to tuck in and get comfortable for the sky-ride from Tampa to Hartford.

A woman settles next to me and we acquaint ourselves with proper distance. "You from down-here or up-there?" she asked. I must have look puzzled. She continued, "I mean are you from down-here in Florida or up there-in Connecticut?" She still had more to say, "I used to be from up-there but I just couldn't stand the winters. My husband and I moved down here to get away from the ice and cold. Horrible stuff. Just horrible. Ungodly. Ice and slush and snish. And the cold. Gads! You people up-there are gluttons for punishment and maybe even a little bit crazy."

I paraded into her chatter. "Perhaps so, but you can't beat New England when it comes to the beauty of each season," I stuck my claim. "Up-there, as you call it, each season has its own distinctive charm and challenge. Each has its own invitation." (I was probably beginning to sound like a preacher.) "My wife's parents retired to Florida," I continued. "We visited one year in the summer and it was unbearable! Can't believe how you or anyone can live with the heat and humidity down-here! I feel sad for people who don't ever get to know the change of the seasons."

That shut it down! We didn't talk again until we were on the ground in Hartford. She smiled kindly as she left, "been a pleasure," she said, "been thinking about what you said. Hope I didn't offend you." And I said, "No, not at all. Hey, thanks for the ride."

Contradiction

In the days before a recent blizzard
someone said, "As long as it's winter
I'd like some *real* snow!"

Soon the winds blew and snow drifts
formed, waist and then shoulder high,
the worst storm in a hundred years.

Snow sculpted the edges of house tops.
Roads closed by order of the Governor
and the whole world was frozen white.

Just about then I heard someone say,
(yes, it was the same someone)
"I *hate* snow! How much longer 'til spring?"

"Do I contradict myself?" Whitman once asked
only to answer, "Very well then, I contradict myself,
I am large, I contain multitudes."

This is the irony and embarrassment of it:
I am the one who spoke,
both times!

Winter: Drifting Paths

A white dust morning
waits for the rising light
to reveal what night
and sky left in wonder -
fourteen inches of snow
on everything.

Branches, railings, rooftops
each bear the shroud
of heaven's crystals;
and covered lawns wait
for first steps and new
markings of fresh beginnings.

And colors, too, as a red
cardinal solitudes the pause,
and blue peeks through
with yellow slivers of sun
proving that trees are
like windows after all.

Most times such moments
of prayer go unnoticed.
But for a brief hesitation,
this time, as winter covered
the world in brilliant array,
I had the sense to look.

"Uphill Journey"   Bloomfield, Connecticut   February 2017

Spring: Intimations of Heaven

I wonder how she knows
which blades of grass to tickle
so the vivid aroma of fresh cut lawn
will rise like a tide of green meadows?

And what of the waters,
waiting ponds and lakes so still,
until wind disturbs the placid surface
sending ripples spreading to the shores?

When precisely is the instant
when afternoon airs blend with
evening cool and her draft causes
the sweet reach for a sweater?

Breeze is holy and mysterious
and, when served with the edges
of spring, delivers the finest intimations
of heaven, right here on earth.

"Just Be Yourself"   Elizabeth Park, West Hartford   June 2013

"Showing Off"   Lancaster, Pennsylvania   July 2018

Summer: Crickets and Cicadas

Long August shadows are just settling,
rich and thick with muted greens
in evening's earlier dark.

Fresh mown grasses embellish the air
with sweet and moist bouquet
as summer waves adieu

and September prepares her part.
Nature's timing never fails
and does not linger.

Her unalterable passing begins the
process of grief for what
I know I will miss:

sweet butter corn and cherry tomatoes
farm-to-table fresh each day;
katydids and cicadas;

bike rides, early and late, in sync with
the cooler air; a kayak gliding
in near-silence;

the drift of summer sleep in napping
increments; the season's ease
and cultural permission to

slow down, take time, taste the day.
These I truly will mourn.
I already do.

"Sweet Summer Snooze"   Iona, Scotland   May 2012

"Ocean's Surging Praise"   Biddeford Pool, Maine   Summer 2021

Autumn: Yellow Blaze and Gold

A few leaves still cling
as stubborn stems hold tight,
but not for long now.

An Autumn breeze
tugs and rustles them free
in airborne dance.

Yellow-blaze and gold,
russet, red, and orange
swirl and ride the wind.

Autumn splendor grows full,
as winter gets ready
in the next room.

Branches appear as
stick-figures against blue sky
and summer covers give way.

Squirrels - feisty and bold
hide acorns for a snowy day.
Meadows and fields mute

as earth's story is told
and life goes underground
and waits first for freezing

only to warm in the soul
of another season,
to begin the cycle again.

"Autumn Stroll"　　West Hartford, Connecticut　　October 2019

Fireside

Few joys eclipse a winter's fire,
kindling full with evening desire,
for huddling warmth and mystical glow
curling up cozy just steps from the snow.

Mystery alights as rising flames prance
evoking some wish to be held in her trance;
as crackle and pop emerge with their song
bidding release of all held forlorn.

Back in the day it took quite a bit,
axes and muscles in clear-driven split;
twigs and logs strategically stacked,
crinkled up paper, the strike of a match.

Much simpler now, no wood in a tote,
but the effortless click of a tiny remote;
no lingering smoke, no fuss and no worry,
as snow on the outside still falls in a flurry.

It's more antiseptic, no cleanup to follow;
no wood to keep feeding or hiss in the bellow.
But this way or that, old way or new,
a night by the fire still whispers her view:

"The day's nearly over, all are now home;
there's shelter and quiet from all left undone.
Sit down, take a load off, it's time to let go.
I'll burn as I will, come, bask in my glow."

"Cold Winters Night"   Saco, Maine   December 2020

This night shot captures something called the Great Conversion from our front yard. It occurs every 800 years when Jupiter and Saturn orbit in close proximity, shining forth a single light in the sky. Its most recent visit was three days before Christmas in 2020. Many people wondered about it being like the Bethlehem Star. It was a perfect night to sit inside by the fire and ponder such large and mysterious thoughts!

Vapor Trails

Half a dozen in one glance aloft some 30,000 feet.
Scattered white lines make their mark on a pallet of blue sky -
vapor trails in close parallel, some crisscrossing others
as they form in the tailwind of large planes
beginning to descend over the southern coast of Maine.

They send soft signals that someone is on the way somewhere,
leaving or landing, going far away or coming back, departing
one port for another. And best guess: in a carry-on
overhead might be a baguette baked in Paris, single malt
distilled in Oban, or fine woolens made by Dublin hands.

And count on this, too. A small boy waits at the gate
for his grandfather's adoring arms; or a soldier returns
to the home soil he loves; maybe a student arrives
for a semester in a country unfamiliar; or a running hug
brimmed with the sweet taste and hope of love's reunion.

Lines across the sky say so much. Coming and going.
Gladness and sadness.   Vapor trails bringing
people together and igniting the soul's longing.
They conjure dreaming and wonder.   I know such things
because, no longer young, I am still that small boy waiting.

"Leaving and Landing"   Scarborough, Maine   August 2021

"The Wings of the Morning"   Saco, Maine   June 2022

Grace Arriving

She arrives in the silence, no need for attention;
knows her own way, expects not a mention.

As colors of autumn in splendorous glance,
and leaves gently fall as if in a dance.

Or a single-voiced choir as a bird with his song,
chirping goodness in winter to hearts long forlorn.

And then in the garden she comes slowly, too,
as bulbs reawaken to springtime's new view.

Or mist-coated moorings of harbor-side ease,
and a pause on the edge of a cool summer breeze.

She comes as she will, this Grace, not for earning,
and offers herself, understanding the yearning.

There's only one catch, very large, also small;
open hearts to receive - no *really*, that's all.

Jigsaw

Something purrs as pieces slip into place

and the sensation of fit is found

among cardboard cutouts,
seemingly random,
creating a larger picture
with order and form,
boundary and definition,
color and shape and
expression as if all to say
in a whisper
of searching relief:

every piece belongs,

nothing is wasted,

nothing is left over.

"Casco Jenga" Harpswell, Maine June 2018

Snow Day

Do you remember the days when snow had no sting,
and winter's deep storms were a wonderful thing?

When "no school today" set everyone free,
so that you could be you and I could be me?

And mittens and snow-pants provided us cover
to plunge into crystal-white-drifts as a lover?

When sledding and sliding were all we were wanting
and Tower Hill waited, so tall and so daunting?

Such thoughts flooded back as I watched in the distance
a gaggle of kids and their laughing persistence;

making angel-wing-etchings and snowballs just so,
and a family of Frosty all lined in a row.

My memory leapt as I basked in their play,
with thoughts of delight just like theirs in my day.

Their romping awakened my child deep within,
and softened my heart for the snow once again.

I will try to remember as the next storm arrives
the call of each day to be fully alive!

Joy Is Like

a puppy romping in the autumn grass
darting quickly in pursuit
of a yellow leaf -
both caught in the swirl of a windy dance.

a small boy at play with his Grampa
splashing the edges of a pond
skipping stones over
the mirrored surface with laughing glee.

a gaggle of birds on the power line,
forming a community of song
each moving over
for yet another feathered soprano or alto.

an ocean breeze on an October day -
or any day for that matter -
carrying breath from
some far away and filling hungry lungs with relief.

So simple, this thing called joy -
so easy and full of yes.
Odd that we humans,
seem to experience it so rarely and sparely.

Kennebunk Air

A single breath is all it takes

for Kennebunk air to revive tired lungs.
The debris of miles and days lift
as sense and soul reawaken together.

Mist and sea set loose archetypal
blessings of restoring power
and healing Atlantic mystique descends

as ocean breezes surround and mend.
This is why the shore beckons me as she does,
and how waves refresh, and salt-air cleanses.

A single breath is all it takes.

"Full Sails Up"   Kennebunkport, Maine   July 2017

"A Burst of Pure Glory"   Lyman Orchard, Maine   October 2022

Autumn Again

There is no such thing
as autumn again, as if
a repeatable season.

There is no recycling
the splendor of colors
or fast moving clouds;

no duplication of
pumpkins and haystacks
or aromas of harvest.

These are moments
of now: fireside smells
and apple tastes,

a chorus of geese
and cool nights
leading soon to winter.

"Behold, I do a new thing,"
the Creative Spirit whispers,
"Do you not perceive it?"

(maybe even wanting to shout)
"That which is here and now
will not ever be seen *exactly so* again!"

Nostalgia

Summer breezes were always fair
and kites rarely crashed as they tugged
their string from the sky.
Do you remember?

Hills were never too steep
that a climb could not overcome
and the view from on top was forever.
Wasn't it just so?

Friendships were for playing
and nothing seemed more complex
than waiting in line for the swing.
Can you recall?

Nostalgia is a mighty force,
a prism that stretches and bends the edges
to better and more than once was.
Or does it, really?

Human hearts and minds are gifts
to hold and behold, and when in goodness
to make hopeful of what might yet be.
Can you imagine?

Woke

It could have just been just luck
that placed me top-shelf and in the sun;
or that some innate qualities and attributes
delivered me with favor over and again.

Some would say that consistent advantage
is born by long effort and a drive to succeed,
or a work ethic instilled, or some superior
blessing planted in secret places.

Of late, though, I am wondering far deeper.
By some visible measure, my white skin
has played an unseen roll, binding me, unaware;
blinding me to an unconscious narrative of power.

Opportunity, home, education, community
have never been denied or in jeopardy for me.
Healthcare, security, and a safe place to be
have all unwittingly played to my benefit.

It might have been another way entirely
than the life of privilege I have known.
It could have been different, and now, at 70,
I am stunned and disturbed to open my eyes.

Packing

I've often wondered why packing up
to go away is such a chore.

Brief stays overnight somewhere
or longer ones with larger time,

the dilemma never seems to change.
Don't take too much! Be sensible!

Best to travel simple and light!
Such advice falls on deaf ears.

The variables are exhausting,
and trying to count them is worse.

What if it's hot? Which camera?
Sunscreen or scarf? And what about?

What will I grimace over, when,
left behind, I should have known?

I am always amazed to get back home
and to discover how much of what

was packed as essential goes back
to the closet, unsoiled, unused!

Beachcomb

Eyes skim in morning light
traces left by waves at night;

ebbing shorelines in her wake,
spoils to find but rarely take.

Some look mostly near the toe,
watching closely, ground below;

while others choose a wider reach
sundry treasures down the beach.

But either way, at toe or wide,
outlook gained by changing tide.

"Tidal Doodles"   Higgins Beach, Maine   July 2021

Seasonal Misery

It drifts in the air and arrives in the nose,
the power it wields only *some* people know.

Pollen, they say, and the mystery of life,
relies on its magic no matter the strife,

of sniffles and tickles of post-nasal drip
or fits of wheezed breathing to gasp and to grip.

At times it is yellow as a dust in the breeze
others not visible still evoking a sneeze.

And eyes itch and scratch with nasal's full flare,
and ears clog and muffle so as not to hear.

There are numbers and metrics ready to weigh
how dense the air is on any given day.

"Air Quality Warning" the forecast reports
cautioning children and vulnerable sorts.

Some call it allergies, others pure hell,
but the mystery of planting reminds us so well:

were it not for the pollen all life would die,
so buck up and bear it with a hanky nearby!

"Everywhere!"   Wounded Knee, South Dakota   July 2014

"Yes, Even in Maine!"   Scarborough, Maine   June 2022

Waiting

Saturday morning
everyone took one
at Seaside Park Bakery.

Tags of paper
numbered the sequence
as we all fell into order.

Oft' times the assembly
wound out the door
clear around the corner

as the aroma of pastry
heightened the stirring
of every anticipation.

Now and again
a friendship began there
or an acquaintance made.

Sometimes it was worth
every minute spent;
other times, not at all.

A looking-glass glimpse,
in line and waiting,
listening for my number.

Preference

I rather enjoy the turn
of a phrase a good bit more
than the completion
of a sentence.

There's a hinge to it,
a word that swings the direction
as if around a corner
to another place.

How many times does
a writer like me pause to wonder
of the most effective way
to express something?

Which reminds me that
my best thoughts don't usually travel
in linear form but as the wind
of an idea suddenly

pulls me to an
unexpected landing, a new bend
I'll gladly navigate as my mind
in curiosity follows.

Whole Body Wags

What quickens the heart more than
a wagging tail at his best friend's return?

Soon the whole-body wags, too: six legs
prancing in delight, scampering for a hug,

as unconditional affection rises all around
and the distance of a day apart vanishes.

Few have mastered the art of welcome
or the salutation of home more completely.

Rich at they who know such secrets, and richer yet,
who share the exuberance of love's reunion.

Yofee, a name meaning "Wonderful"
in Hebrew, filled our lives with love from
December 2002 – April 2018

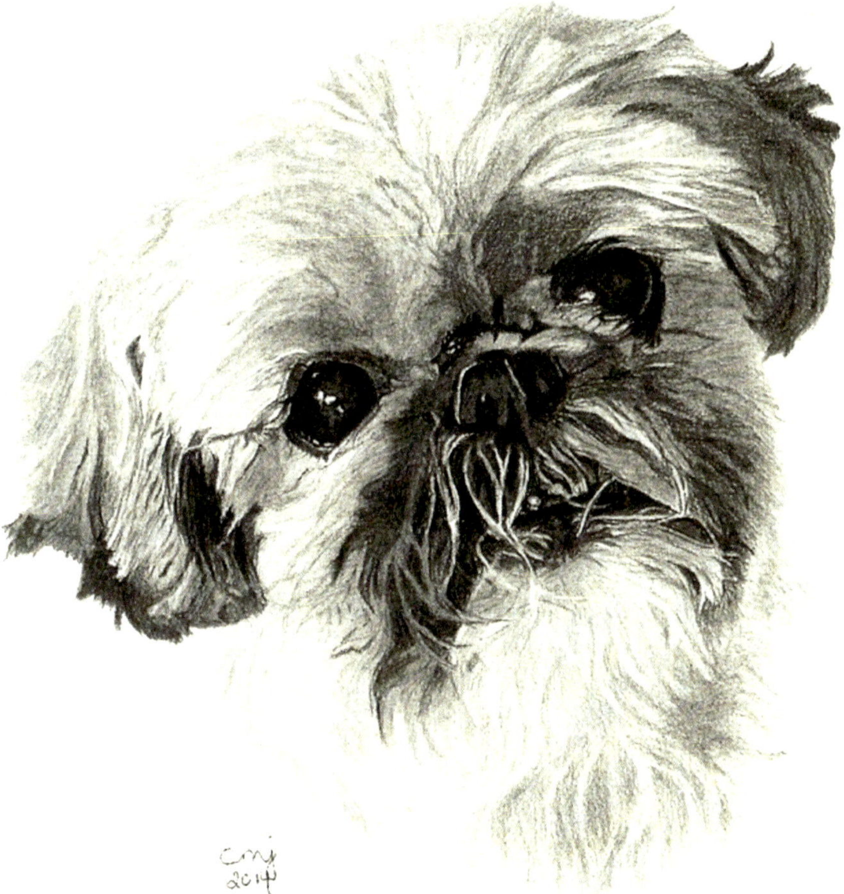
2014

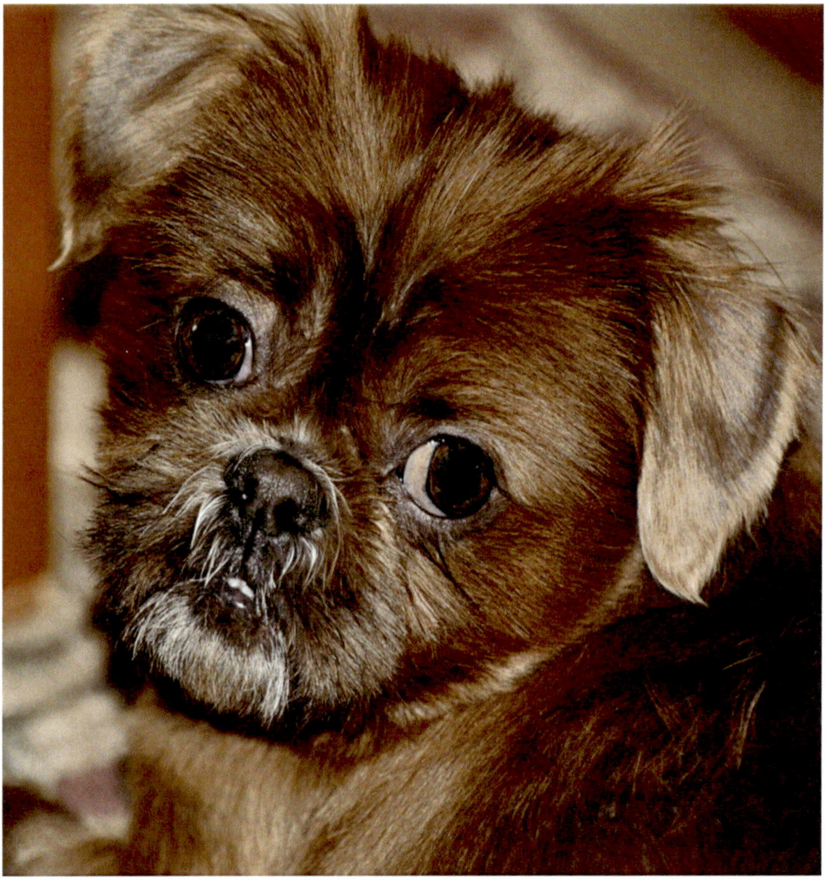

The Moment Is Now

A new creature arrived at our house,
brown-eyed puffball of puppy presence,
barely four pounds, one for each paw,
declaring himself the new owner.

Six days in and his command
on the place has expanded exponentially,
reeling in all who happen by to visit.
The science of imprinting his nascent

mind takes hold, rewarding with treats
the behaviors desired and offering
the steady power of positive reinforcement.
Still to be honest it's not all so clear

who is training whom and whether
it is canine or human ingenuity at work.
Best guess so far: it's a good bit of
both on each side of the growing.

His lessons to date: enthusiasm is
contagious, eye contact is big,
curiosity leads to more, the moment
is now, and love is all there is.

November 23, 2018
Laddie's first week
In his new home with us.

Life Opens Free

A long stretch of living and striving,
of pacing and racing and pushing and driving;
matter less now and almost dissolve
as sixty-plus offers a different resolve.

Life opens free, and quite unexpected,
enhancing the gift with larger perspective,
when most of the rules of an earlier day
seem not as important, at least in this way:

where climbing and earning and achieving and such,
winning and contest lose their old clutch;
noise settles down and clamor much less
questions of age rise to bless.

What is the purpose of life's hard-spent years?
Where is the fruit of the joy and the tears?
And how does one conjure the fury and flatter?
When is it finished, and does it much matter?

"Just this," the voice of wisdom speaks forth,
"the years and the movement all have their worth;
but now is the time to settle and mentor
and to see life's horizon inviting us deeper.

Age speaks in ways that no one could predict,
and offers understanding and acceptance to wit.
Whatever would be if we had solely youth;
and only young growing could offer her truth?"

It Looks Different

now from this end of the field
and not entirely what I anticipated.

I muse back to the day
when contests of endurance,
of hard play and fast movement

set us loose: football, baseball,
racing, propelled at what seemed
like the speed of a rocket

on my young legs, never once
aware those same legs had
limits to them and would olden.

It did not occur, not once, that time
could pass so fast; never seemed
that I would one distant day take

to slowing as my preferred part
and watch from the seasoned
end of the field,
remembering.

"Crossing Over"   Dummerston, Vermont   August 2015

The Other Side

Imagine stepping over a threshold
and then crossing a bridge as life's journey calls
from the other side.

Conjure such crossing as liminal,
a hinge of uncertainty, as familiar ways are relinquished
and new ones are not yet clear.

Drive such thoughts fathoms deeper
as an unseen pandemic converges precisely with departing,
and the world tumbled into collective crisis.

Retirement has plunged me into
such a times as this, blending the wide spectrum of confusion
with my soul's waiting for new leadings.

May the blessing of common ground
descend to each and all of us as we make our various ways
over the threshold and across the bridge to

the other side.

Sabbath Whisper

Every now and again I fall into my soul
as the More of my longing catches its breath
beyond the accustomed pace of my days.

Rest and hope are there, grace and joy, too,
as a wisp of spirit surrounds and lifts me to see afresh
what moments before was muted and tangled.

Self is not at all the master of this place,
and edges are not fixed but fluid
receiving what is both full and empty at once.

Every once and again it happens just so and
time and space conspire as a still voice whispers,
"Hey old friend, good to have you home."

"Sacred Space"   Weston Priory, Vermont   July 2009

"Prayer Filled Sky"   Iona, Scotland   April 2003

This Is the Day

Morning sky spreads out -
blue dotted strings of clouds,
white mostly, but orange with pink
and shadows, too, where dark edges tell of
something I can only guess.

Breeze and crisp air
hold it all together as one;
an eternal canopy hovering
as sun breaks through from behind
bringing warmth and light.

All days bear such awesome
beginnings, all mornings
hold something of magnificence to watch;
but today, by accident of pause
my soul saw what my eyes did.

This is the day that the Lord has made,
I will rejoice and be glad in it!

"Sunrise Over Mull"　　　Iona, Scotland　　　June 2011

In The Leaving

In the leaving, in the letting go,
let there be these
to hold onto at the last:

The delight of surprise.
The fruits of accomplishment.
The whisper of grace.

The power of faith.
The persistence of hope.
The endurance of love.

The experience of purpose.
The arms of community.
The blessing of peace.

For, among you, and as your pastor
you have given these to me,
as I trust you have also received.

Thank you, my beloveds.
Thank you.

(Among my words on my last Sunday in the pulpit of First Church, January 12, 2020.)

*(I am indebted to Jan Richardson for her poem by this title.
I have adapted her words and added to them.
The first strophe is hers; the remaining four are mine.)*

"Next Steps"   Iona, Scotland   June 2011

Increments

When does mist thicken enough to be rain,
or dawn become day, or dusk's shadows turn to dark?
Is there a precise moment when one becomes the other?

Or what of freezing ice-cubes, isolated in trays
as little squares of water, then with forming crystal
edges, and finally completed and solid in the deep center?

Is there ever any clear line of distinction?
And when do the thresholds of childhood become
adolescent, or teenagers morph into emerging adults?

Or what of the passage from middle life to later
when the signs of age become more visible in
the inexorable complexity and mystery common to all of life?

Even the most attentive cannot precisely identify
growing and congealing as exact moments, rather as increments
in the silent processes of life: cyclical some, and others linear.

Still to wonder: Do young ones of every species
youthen and older ones olden?   And do the small changes
toward life's end lead to the More that cannot possibly be seen?

Shelf Life

It's an odd conversation,
a dissonance that begins,
"Oh, didn't you know?

We're not doing that
anymore, changed it
a good while ago now."

It feels like a dismissal
as old ways pass by
before new ones

are even born and the
mastery long learned
is put on the shelf.

So retirement's first lesson:
"Don't take it personally,
it's not about you."

And her second lesson:
"Yes, it is *very* personal.
And yes, it is *exactly* about you."

The Silent Asking

Atlantic magic ensconces
as waves soar and surge
reaching for the sand at Higgins Beach.

Wet droplets of misty ocean
evoke distant times and places,
a different seaside shore of my growing.

Something eternal transcends -
now just as then; inspiring, refreshing,
restoring life beyond any nascent imagining.

"Where were you when
I laid the foundations of the earth?"*
No tepid or benign question by any stretch.

Time holds all human hearts
in the silent asking - we who rely so
on the illusion of our own understanding.

*Job 38: 4

"Awesome Atlantic!"   Biddeford Pool, Maine   June 2020

To Simply Receive

Whispering breezes lead
as sonnets of welcome and farewell
rise from meadows and fields.

Time moves quickly
as the first mist of October arrives
and evening chills call for sweaters.

Earth turns toward autumn
delivering at once glimpses of life and death
through a veil of bittersweet certainty.

Both in arrears and out ahead
summer's ease and play are gone once more
and winter's tasks are making ready.

And in the meantime, this now time,
simply to receive the magnificence
as a season's mirror of the soul.

Yes,
to simply
receive.

"Autumn Air"   McLean Reserve   Granby, Connecticut   October 2012

Harvest at Harpswell

I walk the shore along Casco Bay
as the tides of early day allow.
Lobstermen pull their traps from the sea.
Gulls fly fast and low, diving for breakfast.

My eyes focus on the rocky beach
as I search for tiny white shells,
once holding life, now left behind:
spoils from this harvest at Harpswell.

"More shells like that at Pott's Point,"
a voice instructs. I follow his lead
and find more than plenty
as my backpack fills to overflowing.

A sense of freedom sparked within,
an a'ha moment of delight,
as the accustomed load of distractions
lost their inner grip.

Thoreau once said, "People go fishing
all their lives without knowing it's not the fish
they are after, it's the fishin'."
And so, for me: It's not the shells, it's the shellin'.

"Potts Beach"   Harpswell, Maine   June 2015

"Clear Vision"   Plymouth Notch, Vermont   August 2008

Clarity

The eclipse is imperceptible
as pollen and dust
collect on window panes
in the early spring.

Colors are muted
and details fade
in lost edges
as cataracts obscure.

One hardly notices
such incremental accretions
until the day rags and Windex™
deliver miracles of clarity.

Just so, for the mind,
and also the heart,
clouded without knowing,
yearning to be clear once more.

Watching Over

It was chilly at the gravesite,
damp and translucent
as a thin veil of fog mystified
the reason we had come.

Death does not schedule
with concern for weather,
and the mist that morning
did not stop our need

to bring a loved one to rest.
Ancient words were spoken,
voices calling out to God
as the goodness of a shepherd.

A man watched from the hillside,
appearing oddly surreal to me
as we must also have seemed.
He offered a wave, barely slight,

but enough to make me wonder:
who is this who watches over
such eternal moments?
When all was done I approached

to ask his purpose. He kindly said,
"You do not know me, but I deeply
appreciate the work that you do."
When I turned to look again,

no one was there: only the mist,
and the hillside and the grave, too;
the grave still opened, still fresh
as the fog began to lift.

"Ancient Burial Ground"   Concord, Massachusetts   October 2022

When Life Says No

Once upon a time someone*
sparked this disturbing thought.

"There comes a time when life
says no to some yes in you."

A moment when limitations
form edges and walls

like stone fences around a meadow
that once seemed wide open.

A shoulder's pain, a dimming eye,
the stretch that no longer reaches,

as the inexorable march of time
brings a slow awareness that not

all is as possible as once assumed,
not every urge is a call.

Some would say that wisdom
is learning this truth.

Others just as wise are heard
to mumble "damn!"

> Elizabeth Barrett Browning: "There are times when life says no to some yes in us and the limits of our days begin to close in."

A Deeper More

Retiring comes nearer,
pushing deeper and different.

Moving this time
is much larger than before.

Every prior occasion
was attached to an expansion

of my tomorrows,
advancement in learning,

brand new addresses
and positions in a climb

reaching for mastery
and toward something more.

Carl Jung observed:
"The rules of life's morning

are necessarily different
than the rules of the evening."

I wonder what more
will feel like tomorrow?

I Wonder

what will
become of me
as I relinquish,
the rev and the robe,
the distinction and the role?

So much
and so daily
these have been
one with me and in me,
such that the boundary lines

are on
the far side
of impossible to
discern any longer. Where
do I begin or, for that matter, end?

And how
complete has
the near-total eclipse
of my vocation hidden me
from the deeper nuances of my soul?

These aren't
small wonderings
as the voice of retirement
says, "You must let go now
and trust who you will yet become.

The tides of

life shift later,
just as the autumn breezes
unalterably remind the leaves
to surrender to an unknown path."

"Paths Unknown"   Provincetown, Massachusetts   August 2013

My Lucky Day

I went in for a haircut and got a whole lot more.

For starters no one was sitting in wait before me. The attendant barber, a petite Jamaican woman, smiled as she hummed and motioned me straight-away to her chair. *Something good is about to happen,* I mused to myself. *It just never happens this easy, and with a smile!*

"How are you today?" I asked as I made my way to sitting. Without a pause she said, "Well, honey, I'm just flat-out grateful. I'm plain thankful to God every day. There is no other way to be."

I confess to being stunned some and shy in responding. I was taken by her candor and honesty. And I was convinced that she meant and lived it just as she said. True gratitude cannot, does not lie.

I began to respond in a meaninglessly tepid way about the weather, but before I could find the words, she gave me more of hers. "Isn't the rain wonderful out there? Falling like cats 'n dogs! Everybody is grouchy because of the rain, but not me. I just love the rain. It's like getting blessed from heaven. I do my best work in the rain." And then she laughed, "so honey, this is your lucky day."

She continued humming every snip of the way. What a boost to my spirits. I went in for something so routine as a haircut and received a heartfelt lift such as I hadn't quite experienced in some time.

Rain, shine, or otherwise, may I learn be as grateful as she was along my way. And may I learn to say with each day, and with her lilt and kindness and grace, "Honey, I am flat-out grateful! There is no other way to be!"

"The Wind Blows Where It Will"   Long Island Sound   June 2014

Ruach*

Patience.
Don't panic.
Relax as you might.

Sails
fall limp
as motion fades.

Drift,
anxious waiting
for wind to shift.

Bereft,
abrupt loss
with little left.

Spirit,
whirling Ruach,
not known to quit.

Let go.
Just wait.
The breeze will return.

*Ruach is the Hebrew word
for "the breath of God."

Earth's Turning

A few leaves still cling
but it won't be long now.

Late autumn breezes
chill and rustle them free.

Yellow-blaze and russet,
florescent orange and amber

ride the winds, swirling.
Bare branches silhouette

like charcoal scratches
against a blue pallet of sky.

Hills and fields fall empty
as earth's great story turns

and in a room beyond view
winter hints at coming home.

Life rearranges and hunkers
down, braced and waiting

first for freezing times and snow
only later to thaw in the soul

of another season, growing green
to begin the cycle once again.

"Tree Fort"   West Hartford, Connecticut   September 2016

Birthday Card

Back in the day
Dad was pretty animated about
something called Medicare™
being signed into law.

Little did I understand,
being all of thirteen years,
but later to learn it was mostly about
caring for old people.

Not of much consequence
to a barely teenaged soul with matters
far more compelling like
boats and girls and bicycles.

But seasons pass
and age quickly collects in years
and one recent afternoon the mail presented
me a birthday card in red, white, and blue -

along with a letter explaining
my health benefits an elder citizen.
Seems that thirteen turned into sixty-five
awful darn fast!

Mind Fog

Sometimes my mind feels foggy.
I search for words and find only an edge,
a tip of the tongue kind of thing
but deeper and scarier, too.

What would be left of me if I lost
the expressions of language or thought
on which so much of me depends -
wordsmith that I am?

What if syllable and sound,
coherence and sentence dissolve between
me and another, or worse,
even me and myself?

It frightens me at times
when for the life of me I can't find my keys –
only to discover that they
are in my other hand.

And this is the shadow I fear most.
That one day I will drift to a place wherein
I won't even know that I don't
remember my own name.

Exposure

Light enters
as apertures
open or close.

Higher is small
an orifice,
of tiny measure;

lower opens
wide as more
gleams through.

Combine this
with shutter speed
fractioning

the slice of time
for light to dash in
and have its way.

Quick is essential
as the urgency
of the instance calls.

Then, as the speed of life,
the click signals
a memory preserved.

The Rim of the Day

She rides along
on the rim of dawn
in a melting place where
light pushes darkness away.

She commands
unstoppable power
in sheer cosmic display
of silence and splendor.

Her presence
expanding, stretching
ever higher with a spectrum
of blessing and warmth.

Sunrises: never
two alike, as the veil
of night acquiesces and
makes friends with the day.

A New Tomorrow Dawning

Turning sixty delivered an unexpected perspective I did not anticipate. It honestly took me by surprise. Any who have counted six birthdays ending in zero might understand. This one bore a certain gravity as new horizons appeared in unaccustomed light.

Among all my years collected to date, the expectations of career and vocation have been so defining. Calls and challenges, churches and communities, all there; aspirations and hopes and dreams; accomplishments and hard lessons; and growing, learning and stretching, too.

But something larger was always out ahead and yet to come. Another job to imagine, another mountain to climb, a larger congregation to lead. But now an endpoint comes into view, a finish line of the unknown sort where vocation and economics part ways and a fresh spirit of generativity calls.

There is a wildness to imagine, albeit a tame wildness; a freedom to be and become quite other than the first sixty years have called, with other lives to live and places to name me.

Just to think: even the likes of me at six-decades can dream of a new tomorrow dawning!

"Still Exploring"   Iona, Scotland   June 2012

About the Author

Geordie Campbell retired in 2020 following a beloved vocation as a Pastor in the United Church of Christ. He smiles playfully as he calls *almost* all those years fulfilling and enchanting!

He served forty-two years in various settings, each in the United Church of Christ: Trinitarian Congregational Church in Concord, MA; Newfane Congregational Church in Newfane, VT; South Congregational Church in Granby, CT; and First Church of Christ Congregational in West Hartford, CT. As he retired from a 15-year tenure at his last post he was granted the honorary title of Pastor Emeritus.

His educational credits include Susquehanna University (BA, 1975); Andover Newton Theological School (MDiv, 1980); and Hartford Seminary (DMin 1992). He is an alum of the Spiritual Life Center in West Hartford, CT where he learned the art of Spiritual Direction; and of Auburn Seminary in NYC where he was trained in Executive Coaching.

He and his wife Pam have two grown children and one grandchild. They are delighted to be living along the southern coast of Maine with their shih tzu companion, Laddie.

Ordering Information

Copies of _Glimpses Beyond ~ A Poetic Collection_ are available by direct order from:

>Geordie Campbell
>55 Creeks Edge Drive
>Saco, ME 04072
>860-878-4197
>cgc.pastor.emeritus@gmail.com
>
>Single copy: $18.50
>Shipping: $ 5.00

Also available at the same address are copies of his earlier books. The cost per copy for his earlier work is lower due to the photography included in his newest book.

>Single copy: $ 12.50
>Shipping: $ 5.00

Tell Me with a Story ~ Narrative Prompts for Spiritual Seekers (2022)
As You May Become ~ Living into Faith (2023)